CW00504314

THE **TESTING** SERIES

SPEED, DISTANCE AND TIME
TESTS

THE **TESTING** SERIES

expert advice on interview preparation

Orders: Please contact How2become Ltd,
Suite 2, 50 Churchill Square Business Centre, Kings Hill, Kent ME19 4YU.
You can order via the email address info@how2become.co.uk or through
Gardners Books at Gardners.com.

First published 2011. Revised and updated 2014.

ISBN: 9781907558597

Copyright © 2014 Richard McMunn. All rights reserved.

All rights reserved. Apart from any permitted use under UK copyright law, no part
of this publication may be reproduced or transmitted in any form or by any means,
electronic or mechanical, including photocopying, recording, or any information,
storage or retrieval system, without permission in writing from the publisher or
under licence from the Copyright Licensing Agency Limited. Further details of
such licences (for reprographic reproduction) may be obtained from the Copyright
Licensing Agency Ltd, Saffron House, 6-10 Kirby Street, London EC1N 8TS.

Typeset for How2become Ltd by Molly Hill, Canada.

Printed in Great Britain for How2become Ltd by
Bell & Bain Ltd, 303 Burnfield Road, Thornliebank, Glasgow G46 7UQ.

CONTENTS

CHAPTER 1
WELCOME

Dear Sir/Madam,

Welcome to your new guide: *Speed, Distance and Time Questions*.

Speed, Distance and Time (SDT) questions are used during a small number of technical selection processes to assess a candidate's ability to quickly and accurately carry out often complex calculations in a short period of time.

In many cases, the assessors will require you to perform SDT questions without the use of a calculator and also without the aid of a pen and paper to write down your calculations. They will verbally fire questions at you in rapid succession in order to determine your ability to perform difficult tasks whilst under pressure. It is, therefore, not surprising that SDT questions are used during selection processes for jobs such as pilot within the Armed Forces and similarly the vast majority of HM Forces Officer positions.

I recommend that you work through the examples provided within this guide before working through the large number of sample test questions. The first time you try the tests, use a pen and paper to work out your calculations. It is important that you become conversant in writing down your answers to the questions, and more importantly being able to verify how you achieved the answer. Then, get a friend or relative to sit down with you and ask you each question, only this time verbally. You will need to carry out the calculations in your head, without the aid of pen, paper or calculator. This is far harder to achieve and you may find your success rate drops off. However, this is fantastic practice for any SDT assessment.

One thing I need to stress from the offset is how important it is to be fully conversant and competent in the use of your 12x table. You must be able to carry out multiplication and division quickly in your head, if you are to achieve high scores in any SDT assessment. Remember, not all SDT assessments require you to carry out calculations using a pen and paper. Many of the more technical assessments will require you to perform the calculations in your head. Be prepared for every eventuality.

Whilst I do not want to insult your intelligence, here is the 12x table for you to revise and make reference to:

TIMES TABLE 12 X 12

	1	2	3	4	5	6	7	8	9	10	11	12
1	1	2	3	4	5	6	7	8	9	10	11	12
2	2	4	6	8	10	12	14	16	18	20	22	24
3	3	6	9	12	15	18	21	24	27	30	33	36
4	4	8	12	16	20	24	28	32	36	40	44	48
5	5	10	15	20	25	30	25	40	45	50	55	60
6	6	12	18	24	30	36	42	48	54	60	66	72
7	7	14	21	28	35	42	49	56	63	70	77	84
8	8	16	24	32	40	48	56	64	72	80	88	96
9	9	18	27	36	45	54	63	72	81	90	99	108
10	10	20	30	40	50	60	70	80	90	100	110	120
11	11	22	33	44	55	66	77	88	99	110	121	132
12	12	24	36	48	60	72	84	96	108	120	132	144

Finally, if you are working towards a specific career in the Armed Forces, I have created many books and DVD's on how to pass the selection processes for many different jobs, including RAF, Army, Royal Navy and Royal Marines Officer. You can find out more at:

www.how2become.co.uk

Good luck and best wishes,

Richard McMunn

Richard McMunn

Disclaimer

Every effort has been made to ensure that the information contained within this guide is accurate at the time of publication. How2become Ltd is not responsible for anyone failing their interview as a result of the information contained within this guide. How2become Ltd and their authors cannot accept any responsibility for any errors or omissions within this guide, however caused. No responsibility for loss or damage occasioned by any person acting, or refraining from action, as a result of the material in this publication can be accepted by How2become Ltd.

 THE **TESTING** SERIES

CHAPTER 2
INTRODUCTION TO SPEED,DISTANCE & TIME

In order to be competent in the use of speed, distance and time you must aim for both accuracy and agility. By following this aim you will achieve higher grades during the assessment that you will be required to undertake. During the first part of the guide I will provide you with a tutorial on the most effective way to approach speed, distance and time questions. Having said that, there are alternative methods for tackling the questions, and as such, you should use these if you find them more appropriate to your style of working. During the second part of the guide I will provide you with 20 sample tests, containing a total of 400 questions.

I have already stated the importance of knowing your 12x table. I also recommend that you learn and absorb the following patterns. These will help you to answer the questions faster.

- There are 2 periods of 30 minutes in an hour
- There are 3 periods of 20 minutes in an hour
- There are 4 periods of 15 minutes in an hour

- There are 5 periods of 12 minutes in an hour
- There are 6 periods of 10 minutes in an hour
- There are 10 periods of 6 minutes in an hour
- There are 12 periods of 5 minutes in an hour
- There are 15 periods of 4 minutes in an hour
- There are 20 periods of 3 minutes in an hour
- There are 30 periods of 2 minutes in an hour
- At 60mph, you travel one mile, every minute.

When calculating speed, distance and time questions there are three variables to consider: speed, distance and time. Two of these variables will always be known.

The most effective way to solve these equations is to use the following formulas:

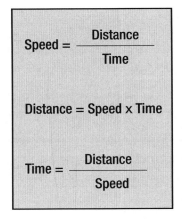

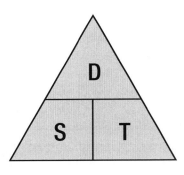

The triangular diagram above is a perfect aid for helping you to memorise the formula. If you place your thumb over the variable you are trying to discover, you will then see the equation required. For example, if I wanted to obtain the time, placing my thumb on T would show that I would need to divide Distance by Speed. When answering questions on speed, distance and time you may find it helpful by starting off writing down the diagram of the triangle at the top.

CALCULATING THE SPEED

Let me provide you with a sample question to work through.

Sample question

What speed covers 30 miles in 2 hours and 30 minutes?

Step 1: We know that the formula required to calculate speed = distance/time.

Step 2: First of all, we must change the time into minutes. If the question was already in minutes, then we would leave it:

2 hours 30 minutes = 150 minutes

Step 3: Speed = 30/150

Step 4: We must now cancel down the fraction until the denominator (the bottom half of the fraction) can be multiplied easily into 60 (minutes).

Speed = 30/150

Speed = 1/5

Step 5: We now need to multiply the denominator (the bottom fraction), until it fits into 60. In this example, the outcome would be 12 – as 5 fits in 60, 12 times.

Therefore, speed = 1 x 12 (5 goes into 60 twelve times)

ANSWER: Speed = 12 mph

Hopefully you found my explanation reasonably clear. I will now provide an alternative method, which is slightly different.

Sample question

What speed covers 34 miles in 10 minutes?

Step 1: If we follow the advice in the previous, we do not need to convert the hours into minutes, simply because it is already done for us.

Therefore, Speed = distance/time

Step 2: Speed = 34/10

Step 3: Calculate how many times 10 goes into 60 minutes. Answer = 6.

Speed = 34 x 6 (6 x 10 =60 minutes)

ANSWER: Speed = 204 mph

CALCULATING THE TIME

The same process for calculating the speed can also be used to work out the time.

Let me provide you with a sample question to work through.

Sample question
How long does it take to travel 48 miles at 20 mph?

Step 1: We know that the formula for calculating time = distance/speed

Time = 48/20

Step 2: Following the same process as the method used to calculate SPEED, the denominator needs to go into 60 (minutes). In this case, 20 will go into 60 three times:

Time = 48/20
(ask yourself, how many times does 20 go into 60 minutes?)

Time = 48 x 3 (3 x 20 = 60 minutes)

Step 3: Time = 144 minutes

Step 4: You now need to convert the 'minutes' into 'hours and minutes'.

ANSWER: Time = 2 hours 24 minutes

CALCULATING THE DISTANCE

Let me provide you with a sample question to work through.

Sample question
How far do you travel in 1 hour and 30 minutes at a constant speed of 40 mph?

Step 1: We know that the formula for distance = speed x time.

Step 2: We also know, therefore, that distance = 40 x 1.5

ANSWER = 60 miles

You can also simply work out this type of question in your head, as follows:

Step 1: At 40 mph, how far do you travel in one hour? The answer is 40 miles.

Step 2: At 40 mph, how far do you travel in 30 minutes? The answer is 20 miles

Step 3: 40 miles + 20 miles = 60 miles

ANSWER = 60 miles

I will now provide you with further explanations of how to answer questions for each of the three parameters. Don't forget to use the triangle to work out the formula required for each question:

Q1. A fire engine travels 60 miles in 3 hours. What is the fire engine's speed?

Formula: Speed = distance ÷ time

Speed = 60 ÷ 3 = 20 mph

Q2. A car is travelling at 30 mph for 70 minutes. What is the distance travelled?

With this problem it is important to remember to work in minutes. This will make it easier to carry out the calculation:

So, 30 mph = 0.5 miles per minute (30 ÷ 60)

70 (minutes) × 0.5 = 35 miles

You can use the formula but you need to convert the minutes into hours and remember that 0.1 = 1/10 of 60 minutes:

Formula: Distance = speed × time

Distance = 30 × 1.1666 (1 hour 10 minutes) = 35 miles

Q3. A tank is driving at 48 mph over 60 miles. How long was it driving for?

Formula: Time =distance ÷ speed

Time = 60 ÷ 48 = 1 hour and 15 minutes

Take these steps:

I. You know that 48 mph = 48 miles in 60 minutes.

II. The difference between 60 and 48 is 12, which is ¼ of 48.

III. You can then take ¼ of 60, which gives you 15 minutes, and add that to 60 minutes = 75 minutes.

IV. Then convert to hours = 1 hour 15 minutes for the answer.

OR

Take these steps:

I. You know that 48 mph = 0.8 miles per minute.

II. 60 ÷ 0.8 = 75 minutes.

III. Convert into hours = 1 hour 15 minutes.

Q4. Rupert cycles at an average speed of 8 mph. If he cycles for 6 and 1/2 hours, how far does he travel?

Take these steps:

> Distance = speed x time
>
> = 8 x 6.5
>
> = 52 miles

Q5. Sally has to travel a total of 351 miles. She travels the first 216 miles in 4 hours.

(a) Calculate her average speed for the first part of the journey.

(b) If her average speed remains the same, calculate the total time for the complete journey.

Take these steps:

> (a) Average speed = distance ÷ time
>
> = 216 ÷ 4
>
> = 54 mph
>
> (b) Time = distance ÷ speed
>
> = 351 ÷ 54
>
> = 6.5 hours

Q6. Susan drives at an average speed of 45 mph on a journey of 135 miles. How long does the journey take?

Take these steps:

> Time = distance ÷ speed
>
> = 135 ÷ 45
>
> = 3 hours

Q7. Jermaine cycles at an average speed of 8 mph. If he cycles for 6 1/2 hours, how far does he travel?

Take these steps:

Distance = speed x time

= 8 x 6 1/2

=52 miles

Q8. Becca has to travel a total of 520 miles. She travels the first 300 miles in 4 hours.

(a) Calculate her average speed for the first part of the journey.

(b) If her average speed remains the same, calculate the total time for the complete journey.

Take these steps:

(a) Average speed = distance ÷ time

= 300 ÷ 4

= ~~54 mph~~ 75mph

(b) Time = distance ÷ speed

= 520 ÷ 75

= 6 h 56 mins

CALCULATING AVERAGE SPEED, DISTANCE AND TIME

You may be asked to calculate the overall average speed of a journey that has multiple legs with different rates of speed. Using the speed, distance and time formula you will be able to find the average speed for a single stage of such a journey.

Calculations that have more than one stage (i.e. a journey where you may have travelled by foot, car and then train) will use the same principle as the calculations listed above; however, you must first consider all the stages. Use the speed, distance and time formula to solve these problems, but remember that you need to add the total speeds, distances or times and divide by the number of stages to calculate the average.

For example: Average Speed = Total Distance ÷ Total Time

Let's work through some examples:

Q1. A traveller visits three cities driving in a triangular route. He first drives from city A to B, 25 miles away, in 1 hour. He then drives from B to C, 20 miles away, in 30 minutes. Finally the traveller then drives from C back to A, 75 miles away, in 1 hour 30 minutes.

$$\textit{Average Speed} = \frac{25 + 20 + 75}{1 + \frac{1}{2} + 1\frac{1}{2}} - \frac{120 \text{ miles}}{3 \text{ hours}} = 40 \text{ miles per hour}$$

Stage	Distance (MILES)	Time (HRS)	Speed (MPH)
A	25	1	25
B	20	½	40
C	75	1½	50
Total	120	3	Average Speed = 40

For example, if distance data was missing from stage B then it could still be calculated using the speed, distance and time formula.

Q2. Judith drives from Plymouth to Southampton, a distance of 160 miles, in 4 hours.

She then drives from Southampton to London, a distance of 90 miles, in 1 hour and 30 minutes. Determine her average speed for each journey.

Take these steps:

Plymouth to Southampton average speed = 160/4 = 40 mph

Southampton to London, time taken = 1 hour and 30 minutes

$$= 1 \text{ and } 1/2 \text{ hours or } 3/2 \text{ hours}$$

$$\text{Average speed} = 90 \div 3/2$$

$$= 90 \times 2/3$$

$$= 60 \text{ mph}$$

Q3. John can type 960 words in 20 minutes. Calculate his typing speed in:

(a) Words per minute,

(b) Words per hour.

Take these steps:

(a) Typing speed = 960/20

= 48 words per minute

(b) Typing speed = 48 x 60

= 2880 words per hour

Now take a look at the following 8 questions, each with a breakdown of how the answer has been reached.

Q4. Peter drives 320 miles in 8 hours. Calculate his average speed.

ANSWER:

$$\text{Average speed} = 320 \text{ miles} \div 8 \text{ hours}$$

$$= 40 \text{ mph}$$

Using the formula:

$$\text{Average speed} = \text{distance} \div \text{time}$$

It is possible to calculate Peter's average speed as shown above.

Q5. Daisy drives from Sheffield to London, a distance of 168 miles, in 4 hours.

Calculate her average speed.

ANSWER:

Average speed = 168 ÷ 4

= 42 mph

Using the formula:

Average speed = distance ÷ time

It is possible to calculate Daisy's average speed as shown above.

Q6. A snail moves 8 metres in 2 hours. Calculate the average speed of the snail in metres per hour.

ANSWER:

Average speed = 8 metres ÷ 2

= 4 metres per hour

Note: The distance the snail moves is measured in metres in this question and not 'miles' as per the other questions. This means that the units used are 'metres per hour' and not 'mph or miles per hour'.

Using the formula:

Average speed = distance ÷ time

It is possible to calculate the snails' average speed as shown above.

Q7. Javinda takes 1 and 1/2 hours to drive 30 km in the rush hour. Calculate his average speed in km/h.

ANSWER:

Average speed = 30 km ÷ 1.5 hours

= 20 km/h

Note: The distance Javinda travels is measured in kilometres in this question and not 'miles or metres' as are all the other questions above. This means that the units used are 'kilometres per hour or km/h' and not 'mph or miles per hour'.

 THE **TESTING** SERIES

Using the formula:

> Average speed = distance ÷ time

It is possible to calculate Javinda's average speed as shown above.

Q8. Rebecca cycles 20 miles on her bike in 2 hours and 30 minutes. Calculate her average speed in mph.

ANSWER:

> Average speed = 20 miles ÷ 2.5 hours
>
> = 8 mph

Note: 2.5 hours is the same as 2 hours 30 minutes because 0.5 of an hour is 30 minutes (half an hour).

Using the formula:

> Average speed = distance ÷ time

It is possible to calculate Rebecca's average speed as shown above.

Q9. Julie can type 50 words in 2 minutes. Debbie can type 300 words in 15 minutes.

Calculate the typing speed of each of the girls in:

(a) Words per minute,

(b) Words per hour.

ANSWERS:

a) Julie's typing speed in words per minute

> Average speed = 50 words ÷ 2 minutes
>
> = 25 words per minute

a) Debbie's typing speed in words per minute

> Average speed = 300 words ÷ 15 minutes
>
> = 20 words per minute

b) Julies typing speed in words per hour

> Average speed = 50 words ÷ 0.0333 hours
>
> = 1,500 words per hour

b) Debbie's typing speed in words per hour

Average speed = 300 words ÷ 0.25 hours

= 1,200 words per hour

Note: To convert 2 minutes into hours simply calculate 2 ÷ 60 to get 0.0333... hours and to convert 15 minutes into hours simply calculate 15 ÷ 60 to get 0.25 which is the same as a quarter (¼). This is why a quarter of an hour is known as 15 minutes!

Q10. Fatima, Emma and Andy each drive from London to Brighton, a distance of 60 miles. Fatima takes 1 hour, Emma takes 2 hours and Andy takes 1 and ½ hours.

Calculate the average speed for each of the drivers.

ANSWERS:

Fatima's average speed:

Average speed = 60 miles ÷ 1 hour

= 60 mph

Emma's average speed

Average speed = 60 miles ÷ 2 hours

= 30 mph

Andy's average speed

Average speed = 60 miles ÷ 1.5 hours

= 40 mph

Q11. Delia drives 220 km in 3 and 1/2 hours. Calculate her average speed correct to the nearest km/h.

ANSWER:

Average speed = 220 km ÷ 3.5 hours

= 62.857 km/h

Rounded to the nearest km, this would become 63 km/h.

Final note:

Remember that if you want your answer to be in the units 'mph' for example, then the numbers you input into the formula should be in 'miles' and 'hours' and not 'kilometres' or 'minutes' for example.

3 SAMPLE HARDER QUESTIONS WITH EXPLANATIONS

Q1. An aircraft flying from London to Madrid is cruising at a speed of 534 mph. The distance from departure is 500 miles and the time remaining to reach Madrid is 1 hour 10 minutes.

What is the distance, in miles, from London to Madrid?

EXPLANATION

500 miles have already been covered by the aircraft, the speed is 534 mph and the time of flight remaining is 1 hr 10 mins = 70 minutes = 70/60 hours.

Distance remaining = Speed x time remaining

= 534 x (70/60)

= 623 miles

Therefore the distance from London to Madrid is 623+500=1,123 miles.

Q2. On a flight from London to Rome the following is shown on the information screen in the passenger cabin.

Current Speed: 822 km/hr

Distance from departure : 1222 km

Time to destination : 22 minutes

What is the distance in kilometres from London to Rome?

EXPLANATION

1222 km has already been covered

distance remaining = speed x time remaining

speed = 822 km/hr,

time = 22m = 22/60 hours

Remaining distance, using:

distance=speed x time

= 822 x [22/60] km = 301.4 km

The total distance between London and Rome, in km's is therefore:

1222+301.4 =1,523.4

Q3. Given that the speed of sound in air is 340 m/s and you hear a clash of thunder 3 seconds after you see the lightning, how far away was the lightning from where you can hear the thunder?

EXPLANATION

Sound travels at 340 m/s from the source of the thunder. If you hear it 3 seconds later that you must use the distance= speed x time formula to calculate how far away you are from the point of thunder. Distance = speed x time

= 340 x 3

=1,020 metres away

Now take the time to work through each of the 20 mock exams that follow.

CHAPTER 3
SPEED, DISTANCE AND TIME MOCK EXAMS

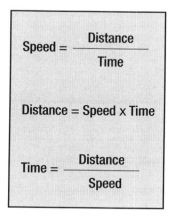

$$\text{Speed} = \frac{\text{Distance}}{\text{Time}}$$

$$\text{Distance} = \text{Speed} \times \text{Time}$$

$$\text{Time} = \frac{\text{Distance}}{\text{Speed}}$$

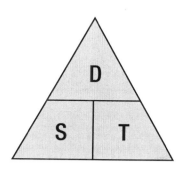

MOCK EXAM 1

There are 20 questions and you have 5 minutes to complete the test. The answers are supplied at the end of the test.

Q1. At 4 mph, how long does it take to travel 1 mile?

ANSWER: | 15 mins   ✓ |

Q2. At 120 mph, how long does it take to travel 60 miles?

ANSWER: | 30 mins   ✓ |

Q3. At 30 mph, how far do you travel in 1 hour and 36 mins?

ANSWER: | ~~45~~ miles (48) (2700) |

Q4. At 1 mph, how long does it take to travel 15 miles?

ANSWER: | 150 hrs |

Q5. At 13 mph, how far can you travel in 1 hour?

ANSWER: | 13 miles |

Q6. At 13 mph, how long does it take to travel 13 miles?

ANSWER: | 1 hr |

Q7. At 19 mph, how long does it take to travel 19 miles?

ANSWER: | 1 hr |

Q8. At 3 mph, how long does it take to travel 11 miles?

ANSWER: | 3 hrs 40 mins |

Q9. At 60 mph, how far do you travel in 1 hour?

ANSWER: | 60 miles |

Q10. At 36 mph, how far do you travel in 15 mins?

ANSWER: 9 miles.

Q11. At 90 mph, how long does it take to travel 12 miles?

ANSWER: 8 mins

Q12. At 15 mph, how long does it take to travel 40 miles?

ANSWER: 2h 40m

Q13. What speed covers 90 miles in 2 hours?

ANSWER: 45mph

Q14. At 165 mph, how long does it take to travel 132 miles?

ANSWER: 48 minutes

Q15. At 19 mph, how long does it take to travel 19 miles?

ANSWER: 1hr

Q16. What speed covers 20 miles in 2 hours?

ANSWER: 10 mph

Q17. At 15 mph, how long does it take to travel 88 miles?

ANSWER: 352 mins

Q18. At 16 mph, how far do you travel in 3 hours?

ANSWER: 48 miles

Q19. At 72 mph, how far do you travel in 25 mins?

ANSWER: 2+5miles 30miles

Q20. At 38 mph, how long does it take to travel 57 miles?

ANSWER: 90 mins

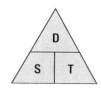

Now check your answers with the ones that follow.

ANSWERS TO MOCK EXAM 1

1. 15 mins
2. 30 mins
3. 48 miles
4. 15 hours
5. 13 miles
6. 1 hour
7. 1 hour
8. 3 hours and 40 mins
9. 60 miles
10. 9 miles
11. 8 mins
12. 2 hours and 40 mins
13. 45 mph
14. 48 mins
15. 1 hour
16. 10 mph
17. 5 hours and 52 mins
18. 48 miles
19. 30 miles
20. 1 hour and 30 mins

Once you are satisfied with your answers, move on to the next mock exam.

MOCK EXAM 2

There are 20 questions and you have 5 minutes to complete the test. The answers are supplied at the end of the test.

Q1. What speed covers 19 miles in 1 hour?

ANSWER: 19 mph

Q2. At 156 mph, how far do you travel in 1 hour?

ANSWER: 156 miles

Q3. At 200 mph, how long does it take to travel 160 miles?

ANSWER: ~~42 mph~~ 48 mph

Q4. What speed covers 36 miles in 1 hour?

ANSWER: 36 mph

Q5. What speed covers 15 miles in 15 hours?

ANSWER: 1 mph

Q6. What speed covers 3 miles in 10 mins?

ANSWER: 18 mph

Q7. What speed covers 8 miles in 24 mins?

ANSWER: ~~3 mph~~ 20 mph

Q8. At 80 mph, how long does it take to travel 140 miles?

ANSWER:

Q9. At 10 mph, how long does it take to travel 10 miles?

ANSWER: 1 hr

Q10. At 170 mph, how far do you travel in 1 hour?

ANSWER:

Q11. At 20 mph, how long does it take to travel 7 miles?

ANSWER:

Q12. At 135 mph, how long does it take to travel 72 miles?

ANSWER:

Q13. What speed covers 18 miles in 10 mins?

ANSWER:

Q14. At 16 mph, how long does it take to travel 12 miles?

ANSWER:

Q15. At 2 mph, how long does it take to travel 19 miles?

ANSWER:

Q16. What speed covers 10 miles in 1 hour and 15 mins?

ANSWER:

Q17. At 16 mph, how long does it take to travel 20 miles?

ANSWER:

Q18. At 18 mph, how long does it take to travel 180 miles?

ANSWER:

Q19. What speed covers 80 miles in 4 hours?

ANSWER:

Q20. At 60 mph, how long does it take to travel 120 miles?

ANSWER:

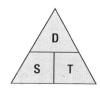

Now check your answers with the ones that follow.

ANSWERS TO MOCK EXAM 2

1. 19 mph
2. 156 miles
3. 48 mins
4. 36 mph
5. 1 mph
6. 18 mph
7. 20 mph
8. 1 hour and 45 mins
9. 1 hour
10. 170 miles
11. 21 mins
12. 32 mins
13. 108 mph
14. 45 mins
15. 9 hours and 30 mins
16. 8 mph
17. 1 hour and 15 mins
18. 10 hours
19. 20 mph
20. 2 hours

Once you are satisfied with your answers, move on to the next mock exam.

MOCK EXAM 3

There are 20 questions and you have 5 minutes to complete the test. The answers are supplied at the end of the test.

Q1. At 80 mph, how far do you travel in 27 mins?

ANSWER: 36 miles

Q2. What speed covers 24 miles in 2 hours and 24 mins?

ANSWER: 10 mph

Q3. At 54 mph, how long does it take to travel 18 miles?

ANSWER: 20 mins

Q4. What speed covers 48 miles in 15 mins?

ANSWER: 192 mph

Q5. At 10 mph, how long does it take to travel 12 miles?

ANSWER: 1 hr 12 mins

Q6. What speed covers 45 miles in 1 hour and 40 mins?

ANSWER: 27 mph

Q7. At 100 mph, how far do you travel in 18 mins?

ANSWER: 30 miles

Q8. What speed covers 2 miles in 20 mins?

ANSWER:

Q9. At 44 mph, how far do you travel in 6 hours and 15 mins?

ANSWER:

Q10. At 5 mph, how long does it take to travel 5 miles?

ANSWER:

Q11. What speed covers 14 miles in 2 hours?

ANSWER:

Q12. What speed covers 15 miles in 2 hours and 30 mins?

ANSWER:

Q13. What speed covers 6 miles in 1 hour and 30 mins?

ANSWER:

Q14. What speed covers 15 miles in 45 mins?

ANSWER:

Q15. At 20 mph, how far do you travel in 3 hours and 15 mins?

ANSWER:

Q16. At 18 mph, how far do you travel in 20 mins?

ANSWER:

Q17. At 16 mph, how far do you travel in 1 hour and 15 mins?

ANSWER:

Q18. What speed covers 2 miles in 40 mins?

ANSWER:

Q19. What speed covers 8 miles in 1 hour?

ANSWER:

Q20. What speed covers 11 miles in 1 hour?

ANSWER:

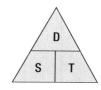

Now check your answers with the ones that follow.

ANSWERS TO MOCK EXAM 3

1. 36 miles
2. 10 mph
3. 20 mins
4. 192 mph
5. 1 hour and 12 mins
6. 27 mph
7. 30 miles
8. 6 mph
9. 275 miles
10. 1 hour
11. 7 mph
12. 6 mph
13. 4 mph
14. 20 mph
15. 65 miles
16. 6 miles
17. 20 miles
18. 3 mph
19. 8 mph
20. 11 mph

Once you are satisfied with your answers, move on to the next mock exam.

MOCK EXAM 4

There are 20 questions and you have 5 minutes to complete the test. The answers are supplied at the end of the test.

Q1. What speed covers 6 miles in 10 mins?

ANSWER:

Q2. What speed covers 25 miles in 10 mins?

ANSWER:

Q3. What speed covers 28 miles in 16 mins?

ANSWER:

Q4. At 10 mph, how far do you travel in 6 mins?

ANSWER:

Q5. What speed covers 14 miles in 1 hour and 24 mins?

ANSWER:

Q6. At 8 mph, how far do you travel in 4 hours?

ANSWER:

Q7. What speed covers 14 miles in 2 hours?

ANSWER:

Q8. At 28 mph, how long does it take to travel 84 miles?

ANSWER:

Q9. At 15 mph, how far do you travel in 1 hour and 20 mins?

ANSWER:

Q10. At 5 mph, how long does it take to travel 16 miles?

ANSWER:

Q11. What speed covers 14 miles in 2 hours?

ANSWER:

Q12. What speed covers 40 miles in 8 hours?

ANSWER:

Q13. At 6 mph, how long does it take to travel 6 miles?

ANSWER:

Q14. At 30 mph, how long does it take to travel 28 miles?

ANSWER:

Q15. What speed covers 15 miles in 3 hours?

ANSWER:

Q16. What speed covers 6 miles in 45 mins?

ANSWER:

Q17. What speed covers 4 miles in 20 mins?

ANSWER:

Q18. At 12 mph, how far do you travel in 2 hours?

ANSWER:

Q19. At 17 mph, how long does it take to travel 17 miles?

ANSWER:

Q20. What speed covers 34 miles in 24 mins?

ANSWER:

Now check your answers with the ones that follow.

ANSWERS TO MOCK EXAM 4

1. 36 mph
2. 150 mph
3. 105 mph
4. 1 mile
5. 10 mph
6. 32 miles
7. 7 mph
8. 3 hours
9. 20 miles
10. 3 hours and 12 mins
11. 7 mph
12. 5 mph
13. 1 hour
14. 56 mins
15. 5 mph
16. 8 mph
17. 12 mph
18. 24 miles
19. 1 hour
20. 85 mph

Once you are satisfied with your answers, move on to the next mock exam.

MOCK EXAM 5

There are 20 questions and you have 5 minutes to complete the test. The answers are supplied at the end of the test.

Q1. At 36 mph, how long does it take to travel 15 miles?

ANSWER:

Q2. What speed covers 57 miles in 9 hours and 30 mins?

ANSWER:

Q3. At 68 mph, how far do you travel in 1 hour?

ANSWER:

Q4. What speed covers 8 miles in 6 mins?

ANSWER:

Q5. At 19 mph, how long does it take to travel 76 miles?

ANSWER:

Q6. At 117 mph, how far do you travel in 1 hour and 40 mins?

ANSWER:

Q7. At 27 mph, how far do you travel in 1 hour and 20 mins?

ANSWER:

Q8. At 8 mph, how long does it take to travel 8 miles?

ANSWER:

Q9. At 6 mph, how far do you travel in 21 hours and 20 mins?

ANSWER:

Q10. At 7 mph, how far do you travel in 2 hours?

ANSWER:

Q11. What speed covers 84 miles in 36 mins?

ANSWER:

Q12. At 16 mph, how far do you travel in 6 hours and 15 mins?

ANSWER:

Q13. What speed covers 19 miles in 1 hour?

ANSWER:

Q14. At 36 mph, how long does it take to travel 120 miles?

ANSWER:

Q15. What speed covers 13 miles in 1 hour?

ANSWER:

Q16. At 9 mph, how far do you travel in 1 hour and 20 mins?

ANSWER:

Q17. What speed covers 15 miles in 12 mins?

ANSWER:

Q18. What speed covers 11 miles in 15 mins?

ANSWER:

Q19. What speed covers 14 miles in 1 hour and 10 mins?

ANSWER:

Q20. At 44 mph, how long does it take to travel 44 miles?

ANSWER:

Now check your answers with the ones that follow.

ANSWERS TO MOCK EXAM 5

1. 25 mins
2. 6 mph
3. 68 miles
4. 80 mph
5. 4 hours
6. 195 miles
7. 36 miles
8. 1 hour
9. 128 miles
10. 14 miles
11. 140 mph
12. 100 miles
13. 19 mph
14. 3 hours and 20 mins
15. 13 mph
16. 12 miles
17. 75 mph
18. 44 mph
19. 12 mph
20. 1 hour

Once you are satisfied with your answers, move on to the next mock exam.

MOCK EXAM 6

There are 20 questions and you have 5 minutes to complete the test. The answers are supplied at the end of the test.

Q1. What speed covers 14 miles in 2 hours and 48 mins?

ANSWER:

Q2. At 15 mph, how long does it take to travel 50 miles?

ANSWER:

Q3. What speed covers 35 miles in 6 mins?

ANSWER:

Q4. What speed covers 36 miles in 2 hours?

ANSWER:

Q5. What speed covers 18 miles in 15 mins?

ANSWER:

Q6. At 48 mph, how long does it take to travel 20 miles?

ANSWER:

Q7. What speed covers 13 miles in 15 mins?

ANSWER:

Q8. At 75 mph, how far do you travel in 1 hour and 8 mins?

ANSWER:

Q9. What speed covers 144 miles in 3 hours and 12 mins?

ANSWER:

Q10. At 20 mph, how far do you travel in 1 hour and 15 mins?

ANSWER:

Q11. What speed covers 42 miles in 2 hours?

ANSWER:

Q12. At 24 mph, how far do you travel in 3 hours and 20 mins?

ANSWER:

Q13. What speed covers 13 miles in 1 hour?

ANSWER:

Q14. At 10 mph, how far do you travel in 2 hours?

ANSWER:

Q15. At 33 mph, how long does it take to travel 55 miles?

ANSWER:

Q16. At 18 mph, how long does it take to travel 45 miles?

ANSWER:

Q17. At 15 mph, how far do you travel in 28 mins?

ANSWER:

Q18. What speed covers 350 miles in 2 hours?

ANSWER:

Q19. At 80 mph, how far do you travel in 54 mins?

ANSWER:

Q20. What speed covers 400 miles in 3 hours and 12 mins?

ANSWER:

Now check your answers with the ones that follow.

ANSWERS TO MOCK EXAM 6

1. 5 mph
2. 3 hours and 20 mins
3. 350 mph
4. 18 mph
5. 72 mph
6. 25 mins
7. 52 mph
8. 85 miles
9. 45 mph
10. 25 miles
11. 21 mph
12. 80 miles
13. 13 mph
14. 20 miles
15. 1 hour and 40 mins
16. 2 hours and 30 mins
17. 7 miles
18. 175 mph
19. 72 miles
20. 125 mph

Once you are satisfied with your answers, move on to the next mock exam.

MOCK EXAM 7

There are 20 questions and you have 5 minutes to complete the test. The answers are supplied at the end of the test.

Q1. What speed covers 4 miles in 15 mins?

ANSWER:

Q2. At 18 mph, how long does it take to travel 36 miles?

ANSWER:

Q3. At 30 mph, how far do you travel in 1 hour?

ANSWER:

Q4. At 26 mph, how far do you travel in 2 hours?

ANSWER:

Q5. At 24 mph, how far do you travel in 7 hours and 20 mins?

ANSWER:

Q6. At 6 mph, how long does it take to travel 15 miles?

ANSWER:

Q7. At 70 mph, how far do you travel in 1 hour and 30 mins?

ANSWER:

Q8. At 7 mph, how far do you travel in 2 hours?

ANSWER:

Q9. At 4 mph, how long does it take to travel 190 miles?

ANSWER:

Q10. What speed covers 5 miles in 5 hours?

ANSWER:

Q11. At 12 mph, how long does it take to travel 3 miles?

ANSWER:

Q12. At 15 mph, how long does it take to travel 14 miles?

ANSWER:

Q13. What speed covers 168 miles in 2 hours and 48 mins?

ANSWER:

Q14. What speed covers 7 miles in 12 mins?

ANSWER:

Q15. What speed covers 102 miles in 36 mins?

ANSWER:

Q16. At 27 mph, how long does it take to travel 18 miles?

ANSWER:

Q17. At 39 mph, how long does it take to travel 52 miles?

ANSWER:

Q18. At 171 mph, how far do you travel in 20 mins?

ANSWER:

Q19. What speed covers 52 miles in 6 hours and 30 mins?

ANSWER:

Q20. What speed covers 84 miles in 42 hours?

ANSWER:

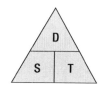

Now check your answers with the ones that follow.

ANSWERS TO MOCK EXAM 7

1. 16 mph
2. 2 hours
3. 30 miles
4. 52 miles
5. 176 miles
6. 2 hours and 30 mins
7. 105 miles
8. 14 miles
9. 47 hours and 30 mins
10. 1 mph
11. 15 mins
12. 56 mins
13. 60 mph
14. 35 mph
15. 170 mph
16. 40 mins
17. 1 hour and 20 mins
18. 57 miles
19. 8 mph
20. 2 mph

Once you are satisfied with your answers, move on to the next mock exam.

MOCK EXAM 8

There are 20 questions and you have 5 minutes to complete the test. The answers are supplied at the end of the test.

Q1. At 17 mph, how long does it take to travel 17 miles?

ANSWER:

Q2. What speed covers 13 miles in 2 hours and 10 mins?

ANSWER:

Q3. At 16 mph, how long does it take to travel 20 miles?

ANSWER:

Q4. At 3 mph, how far do you travel in 2 hours and 40 mins?

ANSWER:

Q5. What speed covers 40 miles in 1 hour and 15 mins?

ANSWER:

Q6. What speed covers 80 miles in 1 hour and 20 mins?

ANSWER:

Q7. At 12 mph, how far do you travel in 15 mins?

ANSWER:

Q8. At 40 mph, how long does it take to travel 24 miles?

ANSWER:

Q9. At 20 mph, how far do you travel in 18 mins?

ANSWER:

Q10. At 57 mph, how long does it take to travel 19 miles?

ANSWER:

11. What speed covers 18 miles in 20 mins?

ANSWER:

12. What speed covers 4 miles in 16 mins?

ANSWER:

13. At 8 mph, how long does it take to travel 12 miles?

ANSWER:

14. At 20 mph, how far do you travel in 2 hours and 24 mins?

ANSWER:

Q15. At 2 mph, how far do you travel in 9 hours?

ANSWER:

Q16. At 25 mph, how far do you travel in 24 mins?

ANSWER:

Q17. At 17 mph, how long does it take to travel 68 miles?

ANSWER:

Q18. At 80 mph, how far do you travel in 1 hour and 3 mins?

ANSWER:

Q19. At 11 mph, how far do you travel in 1 hour?

ANSWER:

Q20. At 14 mph, how long does it take to travel 7 miles?

ANSWER:

D
S | T

Now check your answers with the ones that follow.

ANSWERS TO MOCK EXAM 8

1. 1 hour
2. 6 mph
3. 1 hour and 15 mins
4. 8 miles
5. 32 mph
6. 60 mph
7. 3 miles
8. 36 mins
9. 6 miles
10. 20 mins
11. 54 mph
12. 15 mph
13. 1 hour and 30 mins
14. 48 miles
15. 18 miles
16. 10 miles
17. 4 hours
18. 84 miles
19. 11 miles
20. 30 mins

Once you are satisfied with your answers, move on to the next mock exam.

MOCK EXAM 9

There are 20 questions and you have 5 minutes to complete the test. The answers are supplied at the end of the test.

Q1. At 19 mph, how far do you travel in 1 hour?

ANSWER:

Q2. At 8 mph, how long does it take to travel 20 miles?

ANSWER:

Q3. What speed covers 10 miles in 50 mins?

ANSWER:

Q4. At 3 mph, how long does it take to travel 8 miles?

ANSWER:

Q5. At 6 mph, how long does it take to travel 16 miles?

ANSWER:

Q6. At 12 mph, how long does it take to travel 45 miles?

ANSWER:

Q7. What speed covers 135 miles in 1 hour and 15 mins?

ANSWER:

Q8. At 12 mph, how long does it take to travel 2 miles?

ANSWER:

Q9. What speed covers 42 miles in 3 hours?

ANSWER:

Q10. What speed covers 110 miles in 3 hours and 20 mins?

ANSWER:

Q11. At 100 mph, how far do you travel in 48 mins?

ANSWER:

Q12. At 10 mph, how far do you travel in 3 hours and 36 mins?

ANSWER:

Q13. At 5 mph, how long does it take to travel 56 miles?

ANSWER:

Q14. At 60 mph, how long does it take to travel 12 miles?

ANSWER:

Q15. At 3 mph, how long does it take to travel 10 miles?

ANSWER:

Q16. At 17 mph, how far do you travel in 1 hour?

ANSWER:

Q17. At 4 mph, how long does it take to travel 48 miles?

ANSWER:

Q18. At 8 mph, how long does it take to travel 20 miles?

ANSWER:

Q19. What speed covers 20 miles in 5 hours?

ANSWER:

Q20. What speed covers 11 miles in 5 hours and 30 mins?

ANSWER:

Now check your answers with the ones that follow.

ANSWERS TO MOCK EXAM 9

1. 19 miles

2. 2 hours and 30 mins

3. 12 mph

4. 2 hours and 40 mins

5. 2 hours and 40 mins

6. 3 hours and 45 mins

7. 108 mph

8. 10 mins

9. 14 mph

10. 33 mph

11. 80 miles

12. 36 miles

13. 11 hours and 12 mins

14. 12 mins

15. 3 hours and 20 mins

16. 17 miles

17. 12 hours

18. 2 hours and 30 mins

19. 4 mph

20. 2 mph

Once you are satisfied with your answers, move on to the next mock exam.

MOCK EXAM 10

There are 20 questions and you have 5 minutes to complete the test. The answers are supplied at the end of the test.

Q1. At 12 mph, how long does it take to travel 21 miles?

ANSWER:

Q2. What speed covers 57 miles in 36 mins?

ANSWER:

Q3. At 22 mph, how far do you travel in 1 hour?

ANSWER:

Q4. At 64 mph, how far do you travel in 45 mins?

ANSWER:

Q5. What speed covers 14 miles in 24 mins?

ANSWER:

Q6. At 10 mph, how long does it take to travel 50 miles?

ANSWER:

Q7. At 5 mph, how long does it take to travel 2 miles?

ANSWER:

Q8. At 80 mph, how long does it take to travel 48 miles?

ANSWER:

Q9. At 16 mph, how long does it take to travel 16 miles?

ANSWER:

Q10. At 2 mph, how far do you travel in 1 hour?

ANSWER:

Q11. At 3 mph, how far do you travel in 40 mins?

ANSWER:

Q12. At 16 mph, how far do you travel in 1 hour?

ANSWER:

Q13. What speed covers 9 miles in 20 mins?

ANSWER:

Q14. What speed covers 14 miles in 20 mins?

ANSWER:

Q15. What speed covers 15 miles in 50 mins?

ANSWER:

Q16. At 10 mph, how far do you travel in 48 mins?

ANSWER:

Q17. At 9 mph, how far do you travel in 1 hour and 20 mins?

ANSWER:

Q18. What speed covers 68 miles in 68 hours?

ANSWER:

Q19. At 18 mph, how long does it take to travel 3 miles?

ANSWER:

Q20. At 19 mph, how long does it take to travel 19 miles?

ANSWER:

Now check your answers with the ones that follow.

ANSWERS TO MOCK EXAM 10

1. 1 hour and 45 mins
2. 95 mph
3. 22 miles
4. 48 miles
5. 35 mph
6. 5 hours
7. 24 mins
8. 36 mins
9. 1 hour
10. 2 miles
11. 2 miles
12. 16 miles
13. 27 mph
14. 42 mph
15. 18 mph
16. 8 miles
17. 12 miles
18. 1 mph
19. 10 mins
20. 1 hour

Once you are satisfied with your answers, move on to the next mock exam.

MOCK EXAM 11

There are 20 questions and you have 5 minutes to complete the test. The answers are supplied at the end of the test.

Q1. At 9 mph, how far do you travel in 1 hour and 40 mins?

ANSWER:

Q2. At 64 mph, how far do you travel in 1 hour?

ANSWER:

Q3. What speed covers 168 miles in 6 hours?

ANSWER:

Q4. At 14 mph, how long does it take to travel 14 miles?

ANSWER:

Q5. At 20 mph, how long does it take to travel 72 miles?

ANSWER:

Q6. What speed covers 51 miles in 45 mins?

ANSWER:

Q7. At 95 mph, how long does it take to travel 95 miles?

ANSWER:

Q8. What speed covers 70 miles in 5 hours and 50 mins?

ANSWER:

Q9. At 6 mph, how long does it take to travel 60 miles?

ANSWER:

Q10. What speed covers 36 miles in 1 hour and 20 mins?

ANSWER:

Q11. What speed covers 9 miles in 30 mins?

ANSWER:

Q12. At 40 mph, how far do you travel in 1 hour and 30 mins?

ANSWER:

Q13. At 12 mph, how far do you travel in 1 hour and 15 mins?

ANSWER:

Q14. At 228 mph, how far do you travel in 1 hour?

ANSWER:

Q15. At 64 mph, how long does it take to travel 80 miles?

ANSWER:

Q16. At 9 mph, how long does it take to travel 24 miles?

ANSWER:

Q17. What speed covers 52 miles in 4 hours and 20 mins?

ANSWER:

Q18. What speed covers 20 miles in 30 mins?

ANSWER:

Q19. What speed covers 85 miles in 2 hours and 30 mins?

ANSWER:

Q20. What speed covers 8 miles in 20 mins?

ANSWER:

D
S | T

Now check your answers with the ones that follow.

ANSWERS TO MOCK EXAM 11

1. 15 miles
2. 64 miles
3. 28 mph
4. 1 hour
5. 3 hours and 36 mins
6. 68 mph
7. 1 hour
8. 12 mph
9. 10 hours
10. 27 mph
11. 18 mph
12. 60 miles
13. 15 miles
14. 228 miles
15. 1 hour and 15 mins
16. 2 hours and 40 mins
17. 12 mph
18. 40 mph
19. 34 mph
20. 24 mph

Once you are satisfied with your answers, move on to the next mock exam.

MOCK EXAM 12

There are 20 questions and you have 5 minutes to complete the test. The answers are supplied at the end of the test.

Q1. What speed covers 80 miles in 40 mins?

ANSWER:

Q2. At 14 mph, how far do you travel in 30 mins?

ANSWER:

Q3. At 96 mph, how far do you travel in 1 hour?

ANSWER:

Q4. At 9 mph, how far do you travel in 1 hour and 20 mins?

ANSWER:

Q5. At 20 mph, how long does it take to travel 12 miles?

ANSWER:

Q6. At 6 mph, how far do you travel in 1 hour and 20 mins?

ANSWER:

Q7. At 12 mph, how long does it take to travel 56 miles?

ANSWER:

Q8. At 72 mph, how long does it take to travel 108 miles?

ANSWER:

Q9. What speed covers 152 miles in 4 hours and 45 mins?

ANSWER:

Q10. At 12 mph, how far do you travel in 4 hours and 40 mins?

ANSWER:

Q11. At 90 mph, how far do you travel in 20 mins?

ANSWER:

Q12. What speed covers 19 miles in 1 hour?

ANSWER:

Q13. At 7 mph, how long does it take to travel 7 miles?

ANSWER:

Q14. At 8 mph, how far do you travel in 1 hour and 45 mins?

ANSWER:

Q15. What speed covers 2 miles in 24 mins?

ANSWER:

Q16. At 3 mph, how far do you travel in 2 hours and 20 mins?

ANSWER:

Q17. What speed covers 165 miles in 8 hours and 15 mins?

ANSWER:

Q18. At 12 mph, how long does it take to travel 9 miles?

ANSWER:

Q19. What speed covers 12 miles in 6 hours?

ANSWER:

Q20. At 30 mph, how far do you travel in 2 hours and 24 mins?

ANSWER:

Now check your answers with the ones that follow.

ANSWERS TO MOCK EXAM 12

1. 120 mph
2. 7 miles
3. 96 miles
4. 12 miles
5. 36 mins
6. 8 miles
7. 4 hours and 40 mins
8. 1 hour and 30 mins
9. 32 mph
10. 56 miles
11. 30 miles
12. 19 mph
13. 1 hour
14. 14 miles
15. 5 mph
16. 7 miles
17. 20 mph
18. 45 mins
19. 2 mph
20. 72 miles

Once you are satisfied with your answers, move on to the next mock exam.

MOCK EXAM 13

There are 20 questions and you have 5 minutes to complete the test. The answers are supplied at the end of the test.

Q1. What speed covers 340 miles in 2 hours?

ANSWER:

Q2. What speed covers 120 miles in 3 hours and 20 mins?

ANSWER:

Q3. At 28 mph, how far do you travel in 1 hour and 15 mins?

ANSWER:

Q4. At 12 mph, how long does it take to travel 11 miles?

ANSWER:

Q5. At 40 mph, how far do you travel in 1 hour and 30 mins?

ANSWER:

Q6. At 3 mph, how long does it take to travel 11 miles?

ANSWER:

Q7. What speed covers 30 miles in 10 mins?

ANSWER:

Q8. What speed covers 21 miles in 1 hour and 24 mins?

ANSWER:

Q9. At 10 mph, how far do you travel in 6 hours and 48 mins?

ANSWER:

Q10. What speed covers 48 miles in 24 mins?

ANSWER:

Q11. At 14 mph, how long does it take to travel 7 miles?

ANSWER:

Q12. What speed covers 44 miles in 4 hours and 24 mins?

ANSWER:

Q13. What speed covers 12 miles in 12 hours?

ANSWER:

Q14. At 12 mph, how long does it take to travel 18 miles?

ANSWER:

Q15. At 20 mph, how long does it take to travel 75 miles?

ANSWER:

Q16. At 30 mph, how far do you travel in 1 hour and 48 mins?

ANSWER:

Q17. What speed covers 20 miles in 1 hour and 15 mins?

ANSWER:

Q18. What speed covers 14 miles in 2 hours?

ANSWER:

Q19. At 20 mph, how far do you travel in 3 mins?

ANSWER:

Q20. At 8 mph, how far do you travel in 1 hour and 45 mins?

ANSWER:

Now check your answers with the ones that follow.

ANSWERS TO MOCK EXAM 13

1. 170 mph
2. 36 mph
3. 35 miles
4. 55 mins
5. 60 miles
6. 3 hours and 40 mins
7. 180 mph
8. 15 mph
9. 68 miles
10. 120 mph
11. 30 mins
12. 10 mph
13. 1 mph
14. 1 hour and 30 mins
15. 3 hours and 45 mins
16. 54 miles
17. 16 mph
18. 7 mph
19. 1 mile
20. 14 miles

Once you are satisfied with your answers, move on to the next mock exam.

MOCK EXAM 14

There are 20 questions and you have 5 minutes to complete the test. The answers are supplied at the end of the test.

Q1. What speed covers 9 miles in 1 hour and 48 mins?

ANSWER:

Q2. At 19 mph, how far do you travel in 1 hour?

ANSWER:

Q3. At 60 mph, how long does it take to travel 36 miles?

ANSWER:

Q4. At 15 mph, how long does it take to travel 90 miles?

ANSWER:

Q5. At 40 mph, how long does it take to travel 4 miles?

ANSWER:

Q6. At 1 mph, how far do you travel in 6 hours?

ANSWER:

Q7. At 28 mph, how long does it take to travel 21 miles?

ANSWER:

Q8. What speed covers 16 miles in 1 hour?

ANSWER:

Q9. At 19 mph, how long does it take to travel 19 miles?

ANSWER:

Q10. What speed covers 12 miles in 45 mins?

ANSWER: [   ]

Q11. At 18 mph, how far do you travel in 1 hour?

ANSWER: [   ]

Q12. At 6 mph, how long does it take to travel 14 miles?

ANSWER: [   ]

Q13. At 2 mph, how far do you travel in 4 hours?

ANSWER: [   ]

Q14. At 32 mph, how long does it take to travel 16 miles?

ANSWER: [   ]

Q15. What speed covers 40 miles in 25 mins?

ANSWER: [   ]

Q16. What speed covers 33 miles in 3 hours?

ANSWER: [   ]

Q17. What speed covers 9 miles in 2 hours and 15 mins?

ANSWER: [   ]

Q18. What speed covers 19 miles in 1 hour?

ANSWER: [   ]

Q19. What speed covers 6 miles in 9 mins?

ANSWER: [   ]

Q20. At 18 mph, how long does it take to travel 12 miles?

ANSWER: [   ]

D
S | T

Now check your answers with the ones that follow.

ANSWERS TO MOCK EXAM 14

1. 5 mph
2. 19 miles
3. 36 mins
4. 6 hours
5. 6 mins
6. 6 miles
7. 45 mins
8. 16 mph
9. 1 hour
10. 16 mph
11. 18 miles
12. 2 hours and 20 mins
13. 8 miles
14. 30 mins
15. 96 mph
16. 11 mph
17. 4 mph
18. 19 mph
19. 40 mph
20. 40 mins

Once you are satisfied with your answers, move on to the next mock exam.

MOCK EXAM 15

There are 20 questions and you have 5 minutes to complete the test. The answers are supplied at the end of the test.

Q1. What speed covers 210 miles in 3 hours and 45 mins?

ANSWER: [ ]

Q2. At 30 mph, how far do you travel in 1 hour and 12 mins?

ANSWER: [ ]

Q3. What speed covers 90 miles in 50 mins?

ANSWER: [ ]

Q4. At 192 mph, how long does it take to travel 176 miles?

ANSWER: [ ]

Q5. At 95 mph, how long does it take to travel 95 miles?

ANSWER: [ ]

Q6. At 60 mph, how far do you travel in 12 mins?

ANSWER: [ ]

Q7. At 20 mph, how far do you travel in 9 mins?

ANSWER: [ ]

Q8. At 3 mph, how long does it take to travel 48 miles?

ANSWER: [ ]

Q9. What speed covers 34 miles in 51 mins?

ANSWER: [ ]

Q10. At 11 mph, how far do you travel in 1 hour?

ANSWER: [   ]

Q11. At 8 mph, how long does it take to travel 22 miles?

ANSWER: [   ]

Q12. At 120 mph, how far do you travel in 1 hour and 15 mins?

ANSWER: [   ]

Q13. At 6 mph, how long does it take to travel 70 miles?

ANSWER: [   ]

Q14. What speed covers 3 miles in 9 mins?

ANSWER: [   ]

Q15. What speed covers 18 miles in 18 mins?

ANSWER: [   ]

Q16. At 150 mph, how long does it take to travel 20 miles?

ANSWER: [   ]

Q17. At 17 mph, how far do you travel in 1 hour?

ANSWER: [   ]

Q18. What speed covers 6 miles in 40 mins?

ANSWER: [   ]

Q19. At 9 mph, how far do you travel in 2 hours?

ANSWER: [   ]

Q20. At 12 mph, how long does it take to travel 16 miles?

ANSWER: [   ]

Now check your answers with the ones that follow.

ANSWERS TO MOCK EXAM 15

1.   56 mph
2. 36 miles
3. 108 mph
4. 55 mins
5. 1 hour
6. 12 miles
7. 3 miles
8. 16 hours
9. 40 mph
10. 11 miles
11. 2 hours and 45 mins
12. 150 miles
13. 11 hours and 40 mins
14. 20 mph
15. 60 mph
16. 8 mins
17. 17 miles
18. 9 mph
19. 18 miles
20. 1 hour and 20 mins

Once you are satisfied with your answers, move on to the next mock exam.

MOCK EXAM 16

There are 20 questions and you have 5 minutes to complete the test. The answers are supplied at the end of the test.

Q1. At 15 mph, how far do you travel in 12 mins?

ANSWER:

Q2. What speed covers 195 miles in 1 hour?

ANSWER:

Q3. At 14 mph, how long does it take to travel 14 miles?

ANSWER:

Q4. At 400 mph, how long does it take to travel 60 miles?

ANSWER:

Q5. At 260 mph, how far do you travel in 24 mins?

ANSWER:

Q6. At 70 mph, how far do you travel in 36 mins?

ANSWER:

Q7. At 13 mph, how long does it take to travel 26 miles?

ANSWER:

Q8. At 30 mph, how far do you travel in 1 hour and 10 mins?

ANSWER:

Q9. At 5 mph, how far do you travel in 10 hours?

ANSWER:

Q10. At 19 mph, how long does it take to travel 19 miles?

ANSWER: [   ]

Q11. At 2 mph, how far do you travel in 30 mins?

ANSWER: [   ]

Q12. At 14 mph, how far do you travel in 1 hour?

ANSWER: [   ]

Q13. What speed covers 108 miles in 2 hours and 24 mins?

ANSWER: [   ]

Q14. At 80 mph, how far do you travel in 30 mins?

ANSWER: [   ]

Q15. At 6 mph, how far do you travel in 25 hours?

ANSWER: [   ]

Q16. At 30 mph, how far do you travel in 13 hours and 20 mins?

ANSWER: [   ]

Q17. What speed covers 51 miles in 34 mins?

ANSWER: [   ]

Q18. At 200 mph, how long does it take to travel 60 miles?

ANSWER: [   ]

Q19. At 40 mph, how far do you travel in 21 mins?

ANSWER: [   ]

Q20. At 19 mph, how long does it take to travel 19 miles?

ANSWER: [   ]

Now check your answers with the ones that follow.

ANSWERS TO MOCK EXAM 16

1. 3 miles
2. 195 mph
3. 1 hour
4. 9 mins
5. 104 miles
6. 42 miles
7. 2 hours
8. 35 miles
9. 50 miles
10. 1 hour
11. 1 mile
12. 14 miles
13. 45 mph
14. 40 miles
15. 150 miles
16. 400 miles
17. 90 mph
18. 18 mins
19. 14 miles
20. 1 hour

Once you are satisfied with your answers, move on to the next mock exam.

MOCK EXAM 17

There are 20 questions and you have 5 minutes to complete the test. The answers are supplied at the end of the test.

Q1. At 9 mph, how long does it take to travel 18 miles?

ANSWER:

Q2. What speed covers 13 miles in 1 hour?

ANSWER:

Q3. At 3 mph, how far do you travel in 5 hours?

ANSWER:

Q4. At 18 mph, how long does it take to travel 33 miles?

ANSWER:

Q5. At 5 mph, how long does it take to travel 19 miles?

ANSWER:

Q6. At 3 mph, how long does it take to travel 7 miles?

ANSWER:

Q7. At 15 mph, how long does it take to travel 275 miles?

ANSWER:

Q8. At 192 mph, how long does it take to travel 160 miles?

ANSWER:

Q9. At 8 mph, how long does it take to travel 76 miles?

ANSWER:

Q10. What speed covers 4 miles in 30 mins?

ANSWER:

Q11. What speed covers 85 miles in 2 hours and 30 mins?

ANSWER:

Q12. At 4 mph, how long does it take to travel 20 miles?

ANSWER:

Q13. What speed covers 18 miles in 12 mins?

ANSWER:

Q14. What speed covers 28 miles in 24 mins?

ANSWER:

Q15. What speed covers 20 miles in 30 mins?

ANSWER:

Q16. At 22 mph, how far do you travel in 7 hours and 30 mins?

ANSWER:

Q17. What speed covers 285 miles in 5 hours?

ANSWER:

Q18. At 19 mph, how long does it take to travel 19 miles?

ANSWER:

Q19. At 140 mph, how far do you travel in 30 mins?

ANSWER:

Q20. What speed covers 7 miles in 30 mins?

ANSWER:

Now check your answers with the ones that follow.

ANSWERS TO MOCK EXAM 17

1. 2 hours
2. 13 mph
3. 15 miles
4. 1 hour and 50 mins
5. 3 hours and 48 mins
6. 2 hours and 20 mins
7. 18 hours and 20 mins
8. 50 mins
9. 9 hours and 30 mins
10. 8 mph
11. 34 mph
12. 5 hours
13. 90 mph
14. 70 mph
15. 40 mph
16. 165 miles
17. 57 mph
18. 1 hour
19. 70 miles
20. 14 mph

Once you are satisfied with your answers, move on to the next mock exam.

MOCK EXAM 18

There are 20 questions and you have 5 minutes to complete the test. The answers are supplied at the end of the test.

Q1. At 60 mph, how long does it take to travel 12 miles?

ANSWER:

Q2. At 1 mph, how long does it take to travel 12 miles?

ANSWER:

Q3. At 3 mph, how long does it take to travel 10 miles?

ANSWER:

Q4. What speed covers 9 miles in 1 hour and 30 mins?

ANSWER:

Q5. What speed covers 56 miles in 2 hours and 48 mins?

ANSWER:

Q6. At 4 mph, how long does it take to travel 16 miles?

ANSWER:

Q7. What speed covers 15 miles in 9 mins?

ANSWER:

Q8. At 42 mph, how long does it take to travel 14 miles?

ANSWER:

Q9. At 15 mph, how long does it take to travel 120 miles?

ANSWER:

Q10. At 15 mph, how long does it take to travel 2 miles?

ANSWER:

Q11. At 19 mph, how long does it take to travel 76 miles?

ANSWER:

Q12. At 20 mph, how long does it take to travel 11 miles?

ANSWER:

Q13. At 120 mph, how far do you travel in 22 mins?

ANSWER:

Q14. At 3 mph, how far do you travel in 2 hours and 20 mins?

ANSWER:

Q15. At 1 mph, how long does it take to travel 1 mile?

ANSWER:

Q16. At 12 mph, how far do you travel in 30 mins?

ANSWER:

Q17. At 30 mph, how far do you travel in 1 hour?

ANSWER:

Q18. At 100 mph, how long does it take to travel 180 miles?

ANSWER:

Q19. At 72 mph, how far do you travel in 1 hour and 5 mins?

ANSWER:

Q20. At 54 mph, how long does it take to travel 9 miles?

ANSWER:

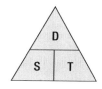

Now check your answers with the ones that follow.

ANSWERS TO MOCK EXAM 18

1. 12 mins
2. 12 hours
3. 3 hours and 20 mins
4. 6 mph
5. 20 mph
6. 4 hours
7. 100 mph
8. 20 mins
9. 8 hours
10. 8 mins
11. 4 hours
12. 33 mins
13. 44 miles
14. 7 miles
15. 1 hour
16. 6 miles
17. 30 miles
18. 1 hour and 48 mins
19. 78 miles
20. 10 mins

Once you are satisfied with your answers, move on to the next mock exam.

MOCK EXAM 19

There are 20 questions and you have 5 minutes to complete the test. The answers are supplied at the end of the test.

Q1. A man is walking along the street at 7 ft/sec. How far will he walk in 57 sec?

ANSWER:

Q2. A train is moving at 40 km/hr. How far will it travel in 6 hr?

ANSWER:

Q3. A man is walking along the street at 3 m/sec. How far will he walk in 53 sec?

ANSWER:

Q4. A deer is running across an open field at 5 m/sec. How far will the deer run in 25 sec?

ANSWER:

Q5. A deer is running across an open field at 3 m/sec. How far will the deer run in 42 sec?

ANSWER:

Q6. A bus is moving along the road at 11 miles per hour. How far will it travel in 7 hrs?

ANSWER:

Q7. An insect is crawling in a straight line at a speed of 3 cm/sec. How far will this insect move in 54 sec?

ANSWER:

Q8. Jim travels 45 miles at 15 mph. How long does it take him?

ANSWER:

Q9. Janet walks at 4 mph for 2½ hours. How far does she walk?

ANSWER:

Q10. Margaret drives at a constant speed. In the first three hours she travels 81 miles. How far will she have travelled after 5 hours?

ANSWER:

Q11. Calculate the distance that you would travel if you drove for 3 hours at 20 mph.

ANSWER:

Q12. Calculate the distance that you would travel if you drove for 8 hours at 60 mph.

ANSWER:

Q13. Calculate the distance that you would travel if you drove for ½ hour at 76 mph

ANSWER:

Q14. Calculate the distance that you would travel if you drove for 1½ hours at 42 mph

ANSWER:

Q15. How long does it take to travel 120 miles at 40 mph?

ANSWER:

Q16. How long does it take to travel 300 miles at 50 mph?

ANSWER:

Q17. How long does it take to travel 240 miles at 60 mph?

ANSWER:

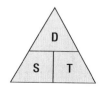

Q18. How long does it take to travel 385 miles at 70 mph?

ANSWER:

Q19. A car travels 300 miles in 5 hours. What is the average speed of the car?

ANSWER:

Q20. Jim can row at an average speed of 2 metres per second. How long does it take him to row 70m?

ANSWER:

ANSWERS TO MOCK EXAM 19

1. 399 ft
2. 240 km
3. 159 m
4. 125 m
5. 126 m
6. 77 miles
7. 162 cm
8. 3 hours
9. 10 miles
10. 135 miles
11. 60 miles
12. 480 miles
13. 38 miles
14. 63 miles
15. 3 hours
16. 6 hours
17. 4 hours
18. 5.5 hours
19. 60 miles per hour
20. 35 seconds

Once you are satisfied with your answers, move on to the next mock exam.

MOCK EXAM 20

There are 20 questions and you have 5 minutes to complete the test. The answers are supplied at the end of the test.

Q1. At 84 mph, how long does it take to travel 112 miles?

ANSWER:

Q2. At 12 mph, how far do you travel in 7 hours and 30 mins?

ANSWER:

Q3. At 9 mph, how long does it take to travel 18 miles?

ANSWER:

Q4. At 10 mph, how far do you travel in 18 mins?

ANSWER:

Q5. At 14 mph, how far do you travel in 30 mins?

ANSWER:

Q6. What speed covers 60 miles in 1 hour and 40 mins?

ANSWER:

Q7. At 15 mph, how long does it take to travel 20 miles?

ANSWER:

Q8. At 4 mph, how far do you travel in 20 hours?

ANSWER:

Q9. At 34 mph, how far do you travel in 1 hour?

ANSWER:

Q10. What speed covers 14 miles in 14 hours?

ANSWER:

Q11. At 5 mph, how long does it take to travel 4 miles?

ANSWER:

Q12. What speed covers 12 miles in 45 mins?

ANSWER:

Q13. What speed covers 11 miles in 1 hour?

ANSWER:

Q14. What speed covers 33 miles in 1 hour and 30 mins?

ANSWER:

Q15. At 18 mph, how long does it take to travel 42 miles?

ANSWER:

Q16. What speed covers 17 miles in 1 hour?

ANSWER:

Q17. At 85 mph, how long does it take to travel 204 miles?

ANSWER:

Q18. What speed covers 14 miles in 4 hours and 40 mins?

ANSWER:

Q19. What speed covers 13 miles in 1 hour?

ANSWER:

Q20. At 16 mph, how far do you travel in 3 hours?

ANSWER:

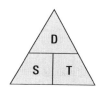

Now check your answers with the ones that follow.

ANSWERS TO MOCK EXAM 20

1. 1 hour and 20 mins

2. 90 miles

3. 2 hours

4. 3 miles

5. 7 miles

6. 36 mph

7. 1 hour and 20 minutes

8. 80 miles

9. 34 miles

10. 1 mph

11. 48 mins

12. 16 mph

13. 11 mph

14. 22 mph

15. 2 hours and 20 minutes

16. 17 mph

17. 2 hours and 24 mins

18. 3 mph

19. 13 mph

20. 48 miles

Once you are satisfied with your answers, move on to the next mock exam.

CHAPTER 4
FINAL MOCK EXAM

During the final mock exam you have 60 minutes to answer the 68 questions. You are permitted to use a calculator if required.

(Give all distances and speeds in whole numbers)

Q1. You are travelling at 28mph for 75 minutes. How far do you travel?

ANSWER:

Q2. You travel 15 miles in half an hour. What speed are you travelling at?

ANSWER:

Q3. You travel 33 miles at a constant speed of 55mph. How long are you travelling for?

ANSWER:

Q4. You are travelling at 80 mph for 1 hour and 30 minutes. How far do you travel?

ANSWER:

Q5. You travel 61 miles in 1 hour and 5 minutes. What speed are you travelling at?

ANSWER:

Q6. You travel 90 miles at a constant speed of 30 mph. How long are you travelling for?

ANSWER:

Q7. You are travelling at 70mph for 125 minutes. How far do you travel?

ANSWER:

Q8. You travel 2.5 miles in 5 minutes. What speed are you travelling at?

ANSWER:

Q9. You travel 75 miles at a constant speed of 45mph. How long are you travelling for?

ANSWER:

Q10. You are travelling at 59 mph for quarter of an hour. How far do you travel?

ANSWER:

Q11. You travel 325 miles in 4 hours and 6 minutes. What speed are you travelling at?

ANSWER:

Q12. You travel 38 miles at 45 mph. How long are you travelling for?

ANSWER:

Q13. You are travelling at 80 mph for 15 minutes. How far do you travel?

ANSWER:

 THE **TESTING** SERIES

Q14. You travel 63 miles in 56 minutes. What speed are you travelling at?

ANSWER:

Q15. You travel 18 miles at 50 mph. How long are you travelling for?

ANSWER:

Q16. You are travelling at 65 mph for one hour and 10 minutes. How far do you travel?

ANSWER:

Q17. You travel 120 miles in two hours. What speed are you travelling at?

ANSWER:

Q18. You travel 80 miles at 50 mph. How long are you travelling for?

ANSWER:

Q19. You are travelling at 40 mph for half an hour. How far do you travel?

ANSWER:

Q20. You travel 80 miles in 1 ¾ of an hour. What speed are you travelling at?

ANSWER:

Q21. You travel 35 miles at 70 mph. How long are you travelling for?

ANSWER:

Q22. You are travelling at 15 mph for 8 minutes. How far do you travel?

ANSWER:

Q23. You travel 16 miles in quarter of an hour. What speed are you travelling at?

ANSWER:

Q24. You travel 60 miles at 55 mph. How long are you travelling for?

ANSWER:

Q25. You are travelling at 30 mph for 10 minutes. How far do you travel?

ANSWER:

Q26. You travel 75 miles in one and half hours. What speed are you travelling at?

ANSWER:

Q27. You travel 1 mile at 60 mph. How long are you travelling for?

ANSWER:

Q28. You are travelling at 50 mph for 2 and half hours. How far do you travel?

ANSWER:

Q29. You travel 100 miles in 1 hour and 55 minutes. What speed are you travelling at?

ANSWER:

Q30. You travel 600 miles at 80 mph. How long are you travelling for?

ANSWER:

Q31. If you travel at 100mph for 2 and half hours, what distance will you cover?

ANSWER:

Q32. You are travelling at 56mph for 1 hour and 6 minutes. How far do you travel?

ANSWER:

Q33. You travel 10 miles in 20 minutes. You then stop for 5 minutes break. You then continue on your journey for a further 20 minutes which covers another 15 miles. What is your average speed?

ANSWER:

Q34. You travel 30 miles at a constant speed of 65mph. You get stuck in traffic for 15 minutes. When you continue your journey, you travel at 45mph for another 10 miles. How long does your journey take you?

ANSWER:

Q35. If you travel at 85mph for 1 hour, what distance will you cover?

ANSWER:

Q36. You leave base at 1023. You arrive at your destination at 1057. You travel 31 miles. What is your speed?

ANSWER:

Q37. You fly towards your Target at 138 mph. You need 1 minute to hit the target. The total distance you cover is 14 miles. What is the duration of your task?

ANSWER:

Q38. You leave base at 1321. You arrive at target A at 1330. You hit target A which takes 1 minute. It takes 6 minutes to reach target B. Again, it takes 1 minute to hit target B. It takes 9 minutes to return to base. You travel at an average speed of 190mph. What distance do you cover?

ANSWER:

Q39. Work is 28 miles from home. You travel at 60 mph for the first quarter of the journey. The remaining journey you travel at 70 mph. What time did you leave home if you arrive at work at 0903?

ANSWER:

Q40. You travel 75 miles at a speed of 70 mph. You stay at your destination for 1 ¾ hours. You then return, travelling at a speed of 80 mph. How long are you away from home?

ANSWER:

Q41. You need to arrive at a destination at 1315. You are 23 miles away. You friend, who live 10 miles away calls you and asks you to wait for them at their house for five minutes so they can ride with you. The route has a speed limit of 50 mph. What time do you need to leave?

ANSWER:

Q42. If you are travelling a distance of 150 miles and aim to complete the journey in exactly two hours , what speed do you need to travel at?

ANSWER:

Q43. You need to arrive at a destination within 5 minutes, you are 8 miles away and it will take you 1 minute to prepare the jet. What speed do you need to travel at?

ANSWER:

Q44. You fly at 200mph, for 185 miles. How long are you flying for?

ANSWER:

Q45. You have half an hour to reach your target, hit it & return. The target is 48 miles away. What speed do you need to fly at?

ANSWER:

Q46. When you reach your destination, you will have covered a total of 320 miles, flying at 195 mph. You had to stop half way through the journey to refuel which took quarter of an hour. What is your total journey time?

ANSWER:

Q47. At 1500, you receive a task to pick up cargo that is 105 miles away. You need to be there and back within the hour. Once you have the cargo, you can travel at a maximum of 180mph. What speed do you need to travel there at?

ANSWER:

Q48. You are carrying cargo which forces you to drive at a maximum of 70 mph. You have to drive the cargo 80 miles. How long will this take you?

ANSWER:

Q49. On Monday mornings, it is your duty to ensure all vehicles all fuelled and clean. There are 5 stops; you spend 20 minutes at each. Each stop is 5 miles apart. The first stop is 23 miles away. You travel at a constant speed of 70mph.

a. What time will you finish at the first stop if you leave at 0630.

b. Assuming you did not stop at any of the stops and left your house at 0630, what distance would you have travelled by 0718?

ANSWER A:

ANSWER B:

50. Work out what time you left, if you arrive at your destination at 1703 and covered 54 miles, travelling at 65 mph.

ANSWER:

For the following questions, the jet's speed will be in knots. Please answer any speed questions in knots, to the nearest whole number. (1 knot = 1.15mph)

Q51. Work out the total distance covered if you are travelling at 202 knots for ¾ hour.

ANSWER:

Q52. You leave base at 1206. You arrive at your destination at 1213. You travel 24 miles. What is your speed?

ANSWER:

Q53. You fly towards target at 138 knots. The total distance you cover is 31 miles. What is the duration of your task?

ANSWER:

Q54. You leave your base at 1902. You are two minutes late. You are supposed to arrive at 2130. You need to cover 55 miles.

a. What speed will you need to travel at to get to your destination by 21:30 if you left at 19:40

b. What speed will you need to travel at to get to your destination on time?

ANSWER A:

ANSWER B:

Q55. You fly for 1 ½ hours at 189 knots. What distance do you cover?

ANSWER:

Q56. You leave your house at 1005. You travel for half an hour at 50 mph. When you reach the motorway, the traffic forces you to drive at 15mph for 12 minutes. After the traffic clears, you continue your journey at 50 mph and arrive at your destination at 1125.

a. How far do you travel in total?

b. How long does the third part of your journey take you?

c. How long would you have been travelling for if you had not got stuck in traffic, assuming you remained at 50 mph the whole journey?

ANSWER A:

ANSWER B:

ANSWER C:

Q57. You are travelling from 0942 to 1158. You travel 190.4 miles. What speed are you travelling at?

ANSWER:

Q58. There are two parts to your journey: for the first part you travel 87 miles at a constant speed of 70mph. You have a rest at the services for quarter of an hour at 1321. You finish the second part of your journey at 1453, travelling a total of 93 miles.

a. How long does the first part of your journey take?

b. What is the total duration of your journey?

c. What speed do you travel at for the second part of your journey?

ANSWER A:

ANSWER B:

ANSWER C:

Q59. You leave your house at 0824. Your journey to work is 21 miles. You usually arrive at 0855. Today, there is slow moving traffic and you are forced to drive at an average speed of 27 mph.

a. What speed do you usually travel to work at?

b. What time will you arrive at work today?

ANSWER A:

ANSWER B:

Q60. You left work at 1703. You arrived home at 1756. You sat in standstill traffic for 21 minutes. You travelled a total of 19 miles. What is your average moving speed? (i.e. excluding anytime you are not moving).

ANSWER:

Q61. At 0822, you and your friend embark on a road trip. You take turns in driving. You drive 134 miles at a speed of 65 mph. You have a pit stop at a service station, and return to the road at 1051. Your friend then drives for 4 hours on cruise control at a speed of 75 mph. You pull into a petrol station and it takes 10 minutes to fill up. You continue for the remaining 165 miles. You arrive at your destination for the night at 1818.

a. How long does the first stage of the journey take, before the pit stop?

b. How many miles does your friend cover?

c. What speed do you drive at the last part of your journey?

d. What is the total distance covered?

e. Who drives for the longest amount of time?

f. Who drives the most miles?

ANSWER A:

ANSWER B:

ANSWER C:

ANSWER D:

ANSWER E:

ANSWER F:

Q62. The distance between yours and Michelle's house is 8 miles. The distance between yours and Ryan's house is 6 miles. Michelle and Ryan live 5 miles apart. You leave your house at 1823 and drive at 40 mph. You then leave Michelle's house at 2003 and arrive at Ryan's house at 2010.

a. What time do you arrive at Michelle's?

b. At what speed do you travel to Ryan's at?

c. What is your average speed for any time that you are driving?

ANSWER A:

ANSWER B:

ANSWER C:

Q63. Your job is 56 miles away. You plan to leave at 0830. You have to be there at 0930.

a. What speed will you need to travel at in order to be there on time?

b. If you wanted to drive at 30 mph, what time would you need to leave?

ANSWER A:

ANSWER B:

Q64. You travel 6 miles and it takes you 6 minutes. You get a flat tire and have to wait 23 minutes for the rescue van to arrive. The van tows you home, which is 20 miles away. He is only travelling 25 mph.

a. At what speed are you travelling before you get the flat tire?

b. How long are you out in total?

ANSWER A:

ANSWER B:

Q65. You are flying to a battle station and receive a call that you need to visit two stop stations in the next half an hour. One station is 23 miles away and the other is 36 miles away. You will be at each stop station for 2 minutes. How fast do you need to travel in order to complete the task?

ANSWER:

Q66. At 0654, you receive a command to fly north for 85 miles. The commander needs you to be in position at 0715. What speed do you need to travel at?

ANSWER:

Q67. You are travelling for 25 minutes. Your speed is 155 mph. You stop for refuelling which takes 3 minutes. You then continue with your journey. Your complete journey covers a total of 119 miles in ¾ hour.

a. How far do you travel before refueling?

b. At what speed do you travel for the second part of your journey?

ANSWER A:

ANSWER B:

Q68. You travel 110 miles at a speed of 66 mph. You stay at your destination for 2 hours. You then return, travelling at a speed of 100 mph.

a. How long is the first part of your journey?

b. How long was your return journey?

c. How long were you away from home in total?

ANSWER A:

ANSWER B:

ANSWER C:

ANSWERS TO FINAL MOCK EXAM

1. 35 miles	**30.** 7 hrs 30 mins	**56.** b) 38 mins
2. 30mph	**31.** 250 miles	**56.** c) 1 hr 12 mins
3. 36 mins	**32.** 62 miles	**57.** 84mph
4. 120 miles	**33.** 33mph	**58.** a) 1 hr 15 mins
5. 56mph	**34.** 56 mins	**58.** b) 2 hrs 47 mins
6. 3 hrs	**35.** 85 miles	**58.** c) 72 mph
7. 146 miles	**36.** 55mph	**59.** a) 41mph
8. 30mph	**37.** 7 minutes	**59.** b) 0911
9. 1 hr 40 mins	**38.** 82 miles	**60.** 36mph
10. 15 miles	**39.** 0838	**61.** a) 2hrs 4 mins
11. 79mph	**40.** 3 hrs 45 mins	**61.** b) 300 miles
12. 51 mins	**41.** 1242	**61.** c) 50mph
13. 20 miles	**42.** 75mph	**61.** d) 599 miles
14. 67.5mph	**43.** 120mph	**61.** e) you
15. 22 minutes	**44.** 55 mins, 30 secs	**61.** f) your friend
16. 76 miles	**45.** 192mph	**62.** a) 18:35
17. 60mph	**46.** 1hr 53 mins	**62.** b) 43mph
18. 1hours 36 mins	**47.** 252mph	**62.** c) 41mph
19. 20 miles	**48.** 1hr 9 mins	**63.** a) 56mph
20. 46mph	**49.** a) 0710	**63.** b) 07:38
21. 30 mins	**49.** b) 56 miles	**64.** a) 60mph
22. 2 miles	**50.** 1613	**64.** b) 1hr 17 mins
23. 64mph	**51.** 174 miles	**65.** 136mph
24. 1 hrs 5 mins	**52.** 179 knots	**66.** 243mph
25. 5 miles	**53.** 12 mins	**67.** a) 65 miles
26. 50mph	**54.** a) 22mph	**67.** b) 191mph
27. 1 min	**54.** b) 30mph	**68.** a) 1 hr 40 mins
28. 125 miles	**55.** 326 miles	**68.** b) 1 hr 6 mins
29. 52mph	**56.** a) 60 miles	**68.** c) 4 hrs 46 mins

 how2become

Visit www.how2become.co.uk to find more titles and courses that will help you to pass any job interview or selection process:

- Online Armed forces testing
- Job interview DVDs and books
- 1-day intensive career training courses
- Psychometric testing books and CDs

WWW.HOW2BECOME.CO.UK

 THE **TESTING** SERIES